Up Holland
in old picture postcards volume 2

by Dr Allan Miller BA, MA, BA, MEd, LCP, DipEd

European Library ZALTBOMMEL / THE NETHERLANDS

ISBN10: 90 288 0954 6

ISBN13: 978 90 288 0954 3

© 1998 European Library — Zaltbommel/Netherlands

© 2010 Reprint of the original edition of 1998

European Library

post office box 49

NL — 5300 AA Zaltbommel/The Netherlands

telephone: 0031 418 513144

fax: 0031 418 515515

e-mail:publisher@eurobib.nl

Introduction

Following the success of the first book 'Up Holland in old picture postcards', it was a pleasant surprise to be asked by the publishers to consider a volume 2. My only reservation was whether it would be possible to obtain a sufficient number of different old postcards. However, I need not have worried; postcards, photographs and papers belonging to the Hunt family were made available to me. For many years the Hunt family lived at The Abbey, previously known as The Priory, next door to Up Holland Parish Church. I am grateful to Mr. Kenneth Hunt's daughter, Mrs. Anne Jones, and her husband, for allowing me access to all the material in the family collection; without it this second volume would not have been possible. Accordingly, this book is dedicated to the memory of the late Kenneth George Hunt.

Until comparatively recent years the character of Up Holland remained essentially unchanged. In 1834 it was described in a Pictorial History of the County of Lancaster as 'one of the most old fashioned looking places, with breakneck streets... It stands on the side of a steep hill, which the streets descend, and where the carriage road zigzags in no manner agreeable.' To escape the squalid scenes of poverty in Wigan during the 'Cotton Famine' of the 1860s, Edwin Waugh rode over the 'green country' to the 'quaint town' of Up Holland to enjoy the 'fine old church' and the 'ivied monastic ruins.' In 1904 newspapers described Up Holland as 'an old world place... a quiet, sleepy village... a place of no small importance... and everything handsome about it.' A visitor in 1926 thought it 'the least spoilt village' in the Wigan area.

Up Holland has a long royal tradition; King Edward II stayed in the village in 1323. To celebrate Queen Victoria's birthday in 1860, children from the village schools went by train to the seaside resort of Southport on what was 'the first treat of the kind'. All subsequent royal weddings and coronations were celebrated in Up Holland. This loyalty was reciprocated in 1935 when Elizabeth, Duchess of York and later Queen of England, came to view the 'Up Holland Experiment', designed to mitigate the social and economic problems of the long-term unemployed in the village.

In addition to high unemployment, Up Holland has had to face a number of other problems. The numerous hills meant that roads were steep in places; 'there are no roads in the country like the Up Holland roads for being rough'. In the 19th century some houses were in a disgraceful state. They were overcrowded and refuse was simply thrown out on to the surrounding land. The drinking water was often obtained from Dean Brook, even though it was not fit for human consumption, 'being much contaminated with refuse and decomposing animal matter'. Serious outbreaks of scarlet fever, measles, diphtheria, typhoid fever and whooping cough were attributed to the 'glaring nuisances of a very offensive nature' in the village. 'No cesspools on the one hand, cesspools full to running over, and no one to empty them, on the other, drains stopped up here, and no drains at all there, offensive matters deposited anywhere from the highway to the back passages, and the houses themselves in a most filthy condition.'

All these aspects of village life presented a challenge to the Up Holland Local Board, which was established in 1872, and, after 1894, to the Up Holland Urban District Council. Mr. Archie Hunt was appointed Clerk of the Up Holland Urban District Council in 1902 and served the local authority until his retirement in 1943. In 1926 his duties were rearranged and extended; he became Clerk, Surveyor, Sanitary Inspector and Valuation Officer for Up Holland. During the early years of the Second World War Mr. Hunt took on extra duties, including fire prevention and civil defence. One of his sons, Kenneth, qualified as a surveyor and worked as assistant clerk to his father until he moved to take up a position with Rochdale Borough Council in 1938. Mr. Kenneth Hunt's love of Up Holland brought him back to live at The Abbey in 1964. Though not a historian by training, he became an expert on the history of Up Holland and his interest in the village led him to assemble an extensive portfolio of written and pictorial records. He and his father were both active in support of Up Holland Urban District Council's effort in the 1920s to acquire and preserve the 17th century Court House in School Lane, with its datestone and connections with the Stanleys, Earls of Derby. Over the years it had served as law court, jail, place of worship and reading room. The intention was to ensure that its character was preserved as a museum for the 'reception and preservation of any ancient curiosities' connected with the village. As part of the conservation campaign the Society for the Preservation of Ancient and Historic Buildings was contacted. Kenneth Hunt's enduring dream was for the whole village of Up Holland to be preserved as a heritage centre. He believed that Up Holland had all the elements necessary for such a designation and these included an ancient church, a long established grammar school and a range of other fine old buildings. He loved the natural beauty of Ashurst Beacon, Dean Wood and Abbey Lakes. He was also fascinated by characters who loomed large in Up Holland's long history; the ancient Holland family, the infamous George Lyon, the Stopford family, and the remarkable Miss Ellen Weeton; Kenneth's father, Archie, was consulted on the publication of Miss Weeton's 'Journal of a Governess'. This volume aims to cover many of the themes, which were dear to Kenneth Hunt in both his public and his private life.

Most of the research for this book was undertaken at the Lancashire Record Office, the Archive Unit of Saint Joseph's College in Up Holland, Wigan History Shop and the Wigan Heritage Archive Centre at Leigh and I am most grateful to the staff for their assistance, support and tolerance. In addition to the Hunt collection, the main sources of information consulted were the Minutes of the Up Holland Local Board, Minutes of Up Holland Urban District Council, local and national newspapers, Up Holland Parish Church Magazines, Saint Joseph's College Magazines and records of the various churches in Up Holland. There is no official History of Up Holland, but Joe Bagley's book 'Up Holland Grammar School' is the next best thing. Christopher Haigh's book 'The Last Days of the Lancashire Monasteries and the Pilgrimage of Grace' contains detailed information on Up Holland Priory in the 16th century and this has been added to by Audrey Coney's research on 'Lancashire's Poorest Monastery'. Jim Sharratt's booklet of 'Up Holland Fragments' remains a mine of information.

Harold and Phyllis Hill willingly allowed me to tap into their expertise and collection of photographs. A scrapbook of newspaper cuttings compiled by Mrs. Edith Dickinson was a most useful source of information; my thanks to her daughter, Mrs. Joan Monks, for allowing me to see it. Other friends, too many to name, made old postcards and photographs available to me, and they have my gratitude. I have to thank my friend Peter Williams for his skill and patience in preparing the photographs for publication. Last, but not least, I need to apologise to my wife, Enid, and my two sons, Simon and Mark, for disappearing to various locations, sometimes for days, whilst I was engaged in the research for this book.

1 The early history of Up Holland is linked to the fortunes of the Holland family. The Hollands were 'among the founders of the Order of the Garter, attended the Royal Family and attained the highest rank in the Peerage'. Robert, Baron Holland, retainer and favourite of Thomas, Earl of Lancaster, became one of the most powerful men in South Lancashire. Nothing exists of the Holland's castle, but the family's legacy remains to this day. The White Lion inn got its name from the crest of the Hollands, which was a white lion rampant on a blue ground. The most lasting memorial is the Parish Church of Saint Thomas the Martyr, which stands on the site of the Chantry founded by Robert Holland in 1307 and which became a Benedictine Priory in 1319; Up Holland Priory was the last Benedictine foundation in England before the Reformation.

THE PARISH CHURCH OF ST. THOMAS THE MARTYR
UP HOLLAND, LANCS.

2   This picture shows a model of the monastery endowed by Robert Holland as an indication of his status, wealth and importance. The Priory was dedicated to Thomas Becket, the patron saint of the Earl of Lancaster. It was endowed with some land in Up Holland, Orrell and Pemberton and was a major agricultural enterprise in the area; pastoral farming predominated, but some corn was grown. Woodland, wildfowl, fish, rabbits and game birds were other resources. In addition to its economic activities, it also supplied the usual religious, community and social functions of a monastery. According to one historian, it obtained extra finance and status as a place of pilgrimage as rich and poor visitors came to view its relics of Saint Thomas. Despite the donations from these pilgrims Up Holland Priory remained Lancashire's poorest monastery.

3   Up Holland Priory was one of the casualties of the Dissolution of the Monasteries in 1536 and only fragments of the original monastic walls, doors and windows have remained. There was no common uprising in support of the monks, but local people did successfully petition for the retention of a chapel for their use, Wigan church being too remote. When Chancellor Tule visited Holland Chapel in 1590 he found a very unsatisfactory state of affairs. There was no Incumbent and there were no books except the 'Common Praier and the Byble which is oulde and torne'. There was 'no communion cup of silver, no chest nor box for the poore.' The Catechism was not used and many received the communion 'that cannot say the Cathecisme'. The register book had not been kept and the 'forfeiture of 12d was not collected from the absents from Church'.

OLD ABBEY UPHOLLAND

4   On the rear wall of the old Court House in School Lane can be seen the Legs of Man symbol; in the 17th century the Earl of Derby from nearby Lathom House was also Lord of the Isle of Man and a supporter of King Charles I. Partly for that reason Up Holland was very staunchly royalist during the civil wars as the teacher, Adam Martindale, discovered. Martindale taught in Up Holland 'not much above a quarter of a yeare' on account of 'many great inconveniences' and 'constant alarmes'. Even though he 'meddled in no side' he was suspected of being a 'Roundhead' (a supporter of the Parliament against the King). His 'habitation in a publick house' was made uncomfortable by 'the soldiers often quartering among us to the depriving us of our beds and chambers'. Adam Martindale was forced out of Up Holland by the troubles of the 1640s.

5 In 1784 Mary Weeton, a widow, with her children Ellen and Tom, moved from Lancaster to Up Holland where 'rents and coals were so much lower'. They lived in 'a pretty cottage elevated from the road by a flight of steps to the front door, and a kind of gallery across the front of the house guarded on the open side by a row of white rails... (and) a pretty little garden on the side of the hill'. The view from the cottage was 'extensive, romantic and beautiful'. The cottage was in Church Street, from where Mary and later Ellen Weeton ran a private school. Ellen kept copies of correspondence and her Journals contain fascinating details of the social life of Up Holland, which she came to hate because of the crime, ignorance, illegitimacy, brutality, intolerance, superstition and scandals.

6   Ellen Weeton left Up Holland in 1808 but was forced to return in 1822. She took lodgings at Garnett Lees, Ball's farm in Newgate on the hillside overlooking Wigan. She occasionally held little tea parties in her 'poky parlour' but life was difficult for her. She was never fully accepted into the social life of the middle class residents of the village. Her health was not good, although she recognised that it was much better than that endured by many villagers: 'Great numbers of them have the Hooping cough and it is very fatal. Many died of it, several children have gone blind with it, some are thrown into fits.' Miss Weeton also thought she knew the cause of much ill health in Up Holland: 'Bread and potatoes were their principal diet. Butter, cream, sugar and pastry, as well as butcher's meat, were rarities but seldom used.'

7 Richard Baxter's clog shop in School Lane was a sort of meeting place in the early years of the 20th century, where young and old used to gather to exchange stories about Up Holland's most notorious character, George Lyon, highwayman. Lyon came to be regarded as a Robin Hood figure; according to some stories he stole the bread out of many a housewife's oven to feed the poor. There are also romantic fantasies about two women in his life, Mary Sloane and Molly Glynn. Other tales relate to a stage coach hold up at Tawd Bridge, his robbery of an excise officer and the attempted shooting of a paymaster. Even the myth makers sometimes admit to his cruelty; during one house burglary he allegedly killed a baby by throwing it into a boiler as the mother hid in terror.

8 This drawing shows where George Lyon's mother lived for part of her life. Lyon himself lived near to the Old Dog Inn and it is possible to obtain an idea of his domestic situation from evidence at his last trial. The road to Lyon's house was 'a narrow passage', out of which there was 'an ascent by several steps to the door'. The passage led to two other dwellings and the door opposite to the steps led to Lyon's house. When the constables entered the house there was no light in the room, except 'a glimmering from the fire' and they found 'another man (Bennett) and a woman were in bed, in the same room' with Lyon sitting on a bed. It was presumably from this house that Lyon worked as a handloom weaver with his apprentice, Luke Bradshaw; perhaps it was the decline of this traditional craft that pushed Lyon into a life of crime.

9 This drawing illustrates the narrow passages in Up Holland, which were the means by which George Lyon and his accomplices, Bennett and Houghton, 'for several years committed the most daring of depredations, and eluded the vigilance of the neighbouring police'. Lyon's life of crime stretched back to his youth; in 1786, aged 25, he was found guilty of 'feloniously apaueling Robert Smith in the King's Highway at the Parish of Wigan and robbing him of Sixteen Shillings', for which he was sentenced to be transported for seven years. The criminal activities of George Lyon and his 'desperate gang' reached a climax in 1814. The neighbourhood had been 'infested with a body of thieves' for months, scarcely a week went by without a burglary. Lyon was the chief suspect and boasted that the rope had not been 'twun' that would fit his neck.

10 The Bull's Head inn in School Lane was where the overconfident George Lyon made mistakes that led to his arrest. In 1814 Westwood House in Ince was robbed; the local constable suspected Lyon and his gang and employed John Macdonald, a 'thief taker' used by the Manchester force, to trap them. Macdonald succeeded in gaining Lyon's confidence by persuading him that he was a dealer in stolen goods. John Baxter, landlord of the Bull's Head, gave evidence that the two had met at his pub and that Lyon had boasted he was 'King of the Robbers'. When Lyon exchanged property stolen from Westwood House for Macdonald's marked bank notes the game was up! At the trial at Lancaster in April 1815, Lyon faced no less than eleven indictments for different robberies and burglaries. The guilty verdict was inevitable and the sentence predictable.

11 On Saturday 22 April 1815 George Lyon, David Bennett and William Houghton were hanged; that 'awful sentence of the law' being carried out 'on the drop behind the Castle of Lancaster'. Simon Washington, landlord of the Old Dog inn, transported Lyon's body to Up Holland; he described it as a traumatic journey because 'the Devil had been with him all the way'. Lyon was buried at the Parish Church 'amidst a concourse of several thousand spectators'. In the early years of the 20th century, Rev. G. F. Wills commented on the steady stream of visitors to Up Holland Parish Churchyard in search of Lyon's grave: 'No shrine or Saint or Martyr could be more eagerly sought than the plain flat stone which does not even bear the name of the man, whose fame seems so altogether out of proportion to his deserts, or even to his eminence as a criminal.'

12 Rev. John Bird, Incumbent at Up Holland Parish Church and teacher, married one of the daughters of Rev. John Braithwaite from The Abbey. During the 1820s The Parsonage was revitalised by Rev. Bird and by the 1840s it was the centre for a group of middle class families whose activities were recorded in diaries kept by Rev. Bird's sister, Mary, later Mrs. Mary Stopford of Bank Top in Roby Mill. Her diaries give a fascinating insight into the social, economic, religious and domestic life of 'Up Holland in the Hungry Forties'. Other families in this circle included the Andertons at The Grove, the Gaskells of Ox House, Dr. and Mrs. Morris from Rock House, the Lythgoes from Holland Cottage and the Holmes of Orrell Hall. There were also contacts with 'strangers' from Southport, Liverpool, Nottingham and Sheffield.

13   The reform of local government in the 19th century led to the establishment of the Up Holland Local Board, which held its first meeting at the Girls' School in Higher Lane on 19 October 1872. Under its Chairman, James Atherton, the Board resolved to appoint a Clerk at a salary of £20 a year, and a Surveyor, an Inspector of Nuisances and a Collector each at a salary of £75 per annum. For its second meeting the Local Board moved to Alma Hill, the premises rented from St. Helens brewers, Greenall, Whitley and Company. The Up Holland Urban District Council came into existence in 1894 with Joseph Basnet as Clerk, a position to be filled in 1902 by Archie Hunt. The Alma Hill site continued to be used, but there were constant complaints about the structural condition of the building and new premises were regularly sought.

14   During the 1920s and 1930s there were proposals to convert the Conservative Club and later the Vicarage into a town hall for Up Holland. However, it was not until after the Second World War that Up Holland Urban District Council moved to its favoured location at Hall Green House with its offices, bowling green and tennis court all on the same site. Until then the local government of Up Holland continued to be conducted from the Alma Hill Council Offices. The Local Board and the Urban District Council were involved in improvements to roads, houses, lighting, health, education, employment and environment. They were actively involved in many of the social activities associated with village life, including leisure, sport and royal celebrations.

15 Up Holland's roads have always presented a variety of problems. The Wesleyan Chapel in School Lane regularly complained about disturbance to the congregation by traffic clattering over the cobbles. Even when the grit setts were replaced by tarmacadam the slippery surface presented a hazard for horse-drawn traffic. During the 1920s the roads in Roby Mill, which were never intended for heavy traffic, were being used by lorries carrying coal from the surface mines at Dalton. Concerned by the serious damage to the roads and the nuisance caused by motor vehicles, the Urban District Council undertook a number of traffic censuses to identify the most affected highways; the census in 1923 revealed that Church Street was used by an average of 291 vehicles per day, many of which were motor vehicles and trailers.

16 The excessive speed of motor vehicles through the centre of the village presented a danger to pedestrians, especially on the congested sections of Parliament Street and School Lane. Heavy steam wagons, often weighing up to five tons and travelling at speeds up to 20 miles per hour, were 'shaking the place to pieces'. This problem was made worse by the dangerous practice of some drivers leaving their vehicles parked on these narrow roads. In 1925 the Council requested the Ministry of Transport to approve a maximum speed limit of 10 miles per hour on these village centre highways, believing that 'four miles an hour is plenty fast enough'.

Other measures included the provision of handrails in Church Street and School Lane to safeguard school children.

17 The hills and corners in Up Holland were particular black spots. There were proposals to close Alma Hill to through omnibus and motor charabanc traffic and to erect boards warning heavy vehicles against using it. Notice boards warned drivers of the exceedingly dangerous corner at the Vicarage. The Northern Manager of the Motor Union felt unable to support Up Holland Council's request for a danger sign to be placed at the top of Bank Brow; it was argued that Bank Brow was not a main road and the local people who did use it would be aware of the hazards. The notorious junction of Parliament Street, Church Street and School Lane was improved by the positioning of a reflector at the top of School Lane to help drivers see vehicles coming from the opposite direction.

18   In the inter-war years, bus and charabanc traffic increased considerably; Up Holland was on a favoured route for pleasure trips to Southport. Relations between Up Holland Urban District Council and local bus companies were often strained. The Council claimed that the buses and charabancs did a great deal of damage to the roads and were a danger to other road users, especially on the narrow stretches of roads in the village. There were also complaints about buses failing to run on time, not stopping at recognised bus halt signs and being overcrowded at peak periods. In addition to the Ribble Buses, other companies recognised the potential of this route including Middleton and Woods Limited, who had been conveying passengers for many years, first in horse buses and more recently in charabancs and motor buses.

19 For years William Webster, a Wigan charabanc owner, had been carrying miners from Up Holland to the Richard Evans and Company's collieries at Haydock. Webster's drivers were warned of the danger of heavy vehicles using Alma Hill because of its steep gradient. They were recommended to use the main road via the Vicarage on all occasions. But it was difficult to negotiate the narrow bottlenecks approaching Church Street in the village and near the Methodist Chapel in Tontine, where the charabancs frequently damaged paving flags. During the 1920s Websters tried to extend their activities in the Up Holland area by offering to serve Crawford and Roby Mill with their latest saloon-type passenger buses; the venture was short lived partly because of lack of passengers from these outlying districts.

20 Mill Lane, leading from the village to Ashurst Beacon, had many attractions, in addition to the old windmill. From there it was possible to see 'the great Sunsetting' in a 'wondrous light of gold, and purple, and triumphant red'. It was a very popular road, but its narrowness presented problems for the Council. In 1920 Wigan Tramway Corporation applied to run buses between the two local beauty spots of Abbey Lakes and Ashurst Beacon during holiday periods, at weekends or whenever there was a festival. However, there were complaints about speeding buses doing damage to the road surface and the footpaths along Mill Lane. More environmentally friendly companies offered to use buses fitted with pneumatic tyres rather than the usual solids.

MILL LANE UPHOLLAND

21 During the 1930s there was a long running dispute about buses stopping in the narrow bottleneck of Parliament Street outside Baxter's store. The road was wider near Rock House and traffic could pass more easily at that point. One resident complained: 'Rock House is the coldest spot which could be chosen, and many colds and much illness can be traced to waiting there for buses which are not always on time. The previous stopping place lower down at the lamp was very much warmer and also shelter could be had when waiting, but now there is none at all, and the north wind sweeps down with full force on unfortunate people who have to stand waiting, and if it rains then the misery is added to... and also the Up Holland District Council owns a building at the previous stop and was quite prepared to make it into a waiting room for buses.'

22 Mr. Lomas filled the oil lamps to light some of Up Holland's highways. In 1878 Wigan Corporation supplied the first gas lamps in Up Holland; two each in School Lane, Parliament Street, Church Street, Hall Green, Alma Hill with one in the centre of the village and another at White Cross Lane. John Swift was appointed as the village lamplighter. But there were regular problems with both the supply and the quality of gas provided by Wigan Corporation; in 1910 the pressure of gas in School Lane was described as 'abominable'. During various coal miners' strikes gas for all street and other public lamps was discontinued to ensure supplies for domestic purposes. A Local Authority survey in 1925 revealed that 535 out of 1,050 householders in Up Holland wanted electricity and in 1931 streetlights were converted from gas to electricity.

23 In the past Up Holland had a plethora of small workshops, including joiners, saddlers, hairdressers, stonemasons, dairies, cowsheds, bakehouses, cloggers, boot makers, wheelwrights and blacksmiths. Sometimes these small scale activities were hazardous. Miss Weeton wrote about a fire at a cabinet maker's workshop which started when sparks fell onto wood shavings; a considerable amount of new furniture was lost and some members of the family were severely burned trying to rescue tools and timber. In 1875 the Council's Medical Officer reported blood, water and refuse running down the gutter on one side of the passage leading to the village slaughterhouse. He recommended various improvements, including a door at the end of the passage 'to shut out all view of the proceedings enacted inside'.

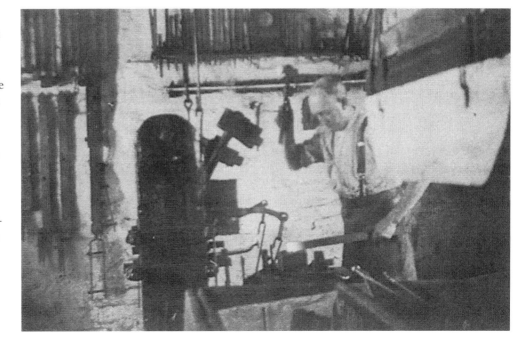

24 Smithying was a long established occupation in Up Holland and the smiths served farms in Up Holland, Skelmersdale and Rainford. Horses were shod and farm implements repaired for more than three hundred years at Alker's smithy in Ormskirk Road. Shod horses from Up Holland took principal prizes at some of the leading agricultural shows in the country. The epitaph of blacksmith Thomas Winstanley, who died on 11 August 1884, aged 71 years, and was buried in Up Holland Parish churchyard, read:

My sledge and hammer is declined
My bellies pipe has lost its wind
My fire decay, my forge extent
And in the dust my vise is laid
My iron is gone, my coals is spent
My nails is driven, my work is done!

25 Itinerant street vendors provided a useful service to the villagers. But there was some concern about 'persons unknown' who were in the habit of meeting school children to solicit rags, in return for which toys were promised. Many street traders advertised their presence by shouting and this became a nuisance. The local Council asked ice cream sellers to discontinue their practice of 'crying' particularly on Sundays. Noise at night was also a problem, especially at weekends, when residents had to endure the disorderly conduct, objectionable language and unruly behaviour of visitors. In 1936 Up Holland Council passed a bye law which stated: 'No person in any street or public place between the hours of 10pm and 6am shall wantonly and continuously shout or otherwise make any loud noise to the disturbance or annoyance of residents.'

26 Carriers also provided a useful service to villagers. Miss Weeton used William Hartley to carry mail and messages and sent her luggage by Anthony Billington's cart. In the late 19th century 'Waring the Mugman' sold all sorts of mugs from his home on Stoney Brow and used his horse and cart to transport quarter casks of ale from Wigan; he was so trusted as a carrier that at least one local family employed him to move glass and china to their new house. Likewise William Fairclough was a trusted village carrier; he met trains at Orrell and Up Holland railway stations and trams at Abbey Lakes to collect parcels, with larger packages transported on a small cart.

The village Carrier UpHolland

27 Up Holland was always a farming village and it once ranked amongst the main market towns of the country with a weekly market held on Wednesdays and an annual fair for horses, cattle and pigs. Up Holland was well located to host such events and had the potential to be 'second to none in any place with an equal population'. However, there was 'something wanting' which prevented Up Holland becoming one of the leading country fairs in the 19th century. There was a good deal of apathy in the neighbourhood; the local landowners in particular did not give their support and it was left to the tenant farmers to keep the show going. With 'a proper social compact amongst the different people of the township' the fair could have brought a great deal of good in the improvement of the agriculture of the district.

28 The Up Holland and District Agricultural Show, held each July at the Abbey Lakes Pleasure Grounds, was very popular and special trams brought great numbers of visitors from the surrounding districts. The show commenced at 11 a.m. and alongside the exhibitions and competitions, bands 'discoursed music' and 'dancing was indulged in'. The most entertaining feature of the afternoon was the jumping competition, which attracted great interest, especially when the riders tackled the water jump. The last event, the donkey race, always aroused great amusement with animals and riders in fancy dress. The animals trotted or walked round the ring, but some of the donkeys took short cuts across the green, showing that 'even the ass knows that the diameter of a circle is considerably shorter than the circumference'.

29   Coal mining was another important economic activity in Up Holland. Its traditional importance was emphasised during the many prolonged strikes. In September 1884 miners at Up Holland collieries were beginning to drift back to work after a strike, which had lasted over four years. This return to the pits was regarded as of great benefit to the neighbourhood because the 'long cessation had been severely felt by all classes'. It was also a very dangerous occupation. In October 1858 one man was killed and two buried alive at Fildes Pit in Pimbo Lane when a shaft collapsed on to them; they were part of a team employed to open the pit, which had closed a year earlier following an explosion of fire damp. Large scale mining in Up Holland ended when the White Moss Colliery closed in 1939 but 'day eye' mines continued to be worked.

30   During the 1920s and 1930s unemployment in Up Holland was often very high, especially during strikes and in periods of economic depression, which affected basic local industries such as coal mining, agriculture and textiles. In 1925 about 2,000 unemployed in Up Holland were signing on at the Unemployment Exchange in the old Up Holland Gardens; many had to queue outside for their dole and they were susceptible to colds and other complaints, because they could not afford to buy enough food. To improve conditions for the unemployed, in 1928, the Ministry of Labour acquired the site for a wooden building on the opposite side of School Lane shown in this picture. In 1935, when more shelter was needed for the men visiting the Unemployment Exchange, an entirely new building was erected on the south side of School Lane.

31 During the long periods of unemployment in the 1920s and 1930s Up Holland Urban District Council obtained government and county council money to support public expenditure on useful township work using the local unemployed and with preference given to ex-servicemen, married men or men with dependants. One major scheme involved the widening of the narrow road near the Cross Keys inn to accommodate the increase of motor traffic and to reduce the risk of accidents at dangerous points. Other schemes included road improvements, building retaining walls, laying of electricity cables and sewer construction in Parliament Street, Church Street, Grove Road, Dingle Road, College Road and Lafford Lane.

32 This picture illustrates many of the social and economic conditions prevailing in the two decades before the Second World War. The high levels of unemployment created conditions of poverty and despair for many families, especially those dependent on coal mining. Because of the Council's efforts, finance was invested in projects designed to benefit the community in general and the unemployed in particular. These schemes of road construction and improvement were labour intensive; the workers employed on this particular project used techniques and equipment employed in the mines, using their manual strength to fill tubs running on tracks with the horse providing mobility. Despite these extraordinary efforts many men were still dependent on the dole and some greater initiative was needed in Up Holland.

33 On Tuesday, 9 July 1935, Elizabeth, Duchess of York, visited the experimental scheme at Lawns Farm to assist the unemployed of Up Holland. Several acres of land and a number of buildings were purchased by the Society of Friends to provide alternative work for miners and cotton workers, and especially older employees with little prospect of finding new jobs. Subsistence farming was the core of the experiment; pigs, poultry, cattle, bees, vegetables and fruits provided food for the participants and were the basis of small scale industries like jam and bread making. Products were not for sale, but those engaged on the project could barter their goods and services at the communal store. Up Holland Urban District Council supplied water for drinking, jam making and sterilising milk bottles.

34 The Up Holland experiment was reckoned to be a success; the Quakers who devised the scheme were overwhelmed with applicants. The Duchess of York took a lively interest as the project was explained to her by Peter Scott, the organiser, on a tour of the site and hoped it would continue to prosper. But it was always small scale; there was no government involvement and even the Society of Friends did not look upon it as a solution to the unemployment problem. However, participants did benefit from the self-help experiment because it meant more food and goods were available, their standard of living improved, there was an opportunity to train for jobs and it supplemented dole money. Perhaps the most important advantage of the project was social: 'Each day brings its duty and its promise of reward in place of vacant and valueless hours.'

35   Up Holland's housing stock contained dilapidated and insanitary houses and blocks of property. Alma Hill, Higher Lane, Tontine and Crawford were particular black spots. During the First World War the sanitary condition of 28 cottages at Crawford was declared to be the worst of any in the village on account of the deplorable condition of their unpaved yards and open ashpits. It was hoped that the conversion of privies to water closets would do away with the objectionable practice of emptying the contents of privies and ashpits on to carts. In 1930 easily the worst property was opposite the Council Offices; scarcely a cottage from Alma Hill to Factory Row was fit for human habitation. In such conditions disease and deaths were never far away; infant mortality in Up Holland was much higher than in other areas.

36   Before their demolition in the 1930s, poor houses on Alma Hill presented particular problems. Many of them had been lodging houses used by itinerant workers, many from Ireland, seeking employment on local farms. In the 19th century the government tried to regulate such establishments by the Common Lodging House Act, but there were many breaches of the law in Up Holland. In 1854 one man had ten persons sleeping in his house on the same night, even though it was not registered as a lodging house. Another man had the same number of people in his 'exceedingly filthy' unregistered lodging house. In a third unregistered house two men were sharing the same bedroom as the proprietor and his wife. Sometimes it was the proprietor who suffered; in 1882 one female lodging housekeeper was robbed of money by a man and his seven year old son.

37   Until his death in February 1885 Brooklands House was the home of Dr. J.L. Molyneux, the Medical Officer of Health for Up Holland; he and his successor, Dr. Browne, presented graphic reports on parts of the village. In 1885 some conditions were 'entirely subversive of the ordinary laws of health'. There was evidence of 'defective drainage, slovenly kept ashpits, unclean closets, foul pig styes, the promiscuous throwing of refuse liquids, and the want of water for washing and slopping purposes'. In other parts of Up Holland the state of the sanitary arrangements 'almost baffles description'. Many of the ashpits were in a broken-down condition and the contents of the closets were discharged into them in a way that was 'simply disgusting'. All the elements necessary for an outbreak of disease were present 'in a very aggregated form'.

38 There was a heavy demand for water by local industries such as Ravenhead and Pimbo Lane brickworks, Grove Laundry, Silver Sands Company, Mountain Mine Company, White Moss Colliery and Crawford Sewage Works. The quality of domestic supplies was often a problem. In 1879 blood from the Newgate slaughterhouse was polluting the domestic water supplies at Up Holland Moor. In 1885 the water in the pump at Crawford was unfit for drinking purposes because there were indications of sewage contamination and the water from the Tontine pump was 'just a little better than barely fit to drink'. A Council survey of private wells in 1910 found the water in some was 'good' but sometimes the supply dried up in summer; in others the quality of the water was 'suspicious' with an indication of sewage contamination.

39 Rats were a problem in the village. Miss Weeton went on expeditions in search of what she called the 'politest brutes'. Up Holland Urban District Council used the Dingle as a storage depot and tip and it was a prime location for rats. The Council organised several campaigns for the destruction of pests. During the First World War head teachers of schools in Up Holland were encouraged to allow their older pupils to destroy rats, house sparrows and green linnets. A responsible farmer in each part of the district was deputed to examine and to reimburse those who undertook extermination of pests on the following scale: rats' tails, per dozen, 1 shilling; heads of fully fledged house sparrows, per dozen, 3 pennies; heads of unfledged house sparrows, per dozen, 2 pennies; house sparrows' eggs, per dozen, 1 penny.

40 The Local Authority took action to remove blackspots from the village by demolishing unsightly buildings. Walker's property at the top of School Lane was removed to improve the appearance of the village. The Alma Hill and Higher Lane part of the village was made a clearance area; the former lodging houses were unsuitable for the purpose, both from a moral and a sanitary standpoint. Other property was knocked down in the name of progress. In 1903 the old corn mill in Roby Mill was found to be in a dangerous state when it was planned to widen and raise the road at that point. Likewise property in Parliament Street and Church Street was demolished to extend the width of the roads; the ghost house was a casualty of such a scheme in 1934.

41 To replace derelict property, to relieve overcrowding in homes and to overcome the housing shortages, Up Holland Council responded positively to initiatives designed to satisfy the demand for suitable houses. On the eve of the First World War a scheme for 35 new workmen's cottages in the village was planned and costed. Following the war other housing schemes were considered at a variety of locations, including Sandbrook Road, Roby Mill, Hall Green and Pimbo Lane. At the same time the Council discussed the possibility of a scheme on the land surrounded by School Lane, Church Street, Tontine Road and the Abbey Lakes Estate.

This proposal involved the area being laid out and developed on town planning lines, which would have been to the 'very great advantage to the district'.

MODEL COTTAGES
SANDBROOK ROAD, UPHOLLAND

42 When snow fell in Up Holland 'skating was freely indulged in, the Abbey Lakes being highly patronised'. In 1880 plans to make Abbey Lakes into an 'improving place for pleasure seekers' were nearing completion. On Whit Monday holiday several thousand people came to enjoy the facilities. A steamboat carried a hundred passengers round the enlarged lake and thirty small pleasure boats were also available. A Grand Gala and Sports featured horse trotting, galloping races, tug of war and foot races. Whilst the children enjoyed the swing boats and other amusements, the adults made use of the excellent bowling green. An 'exotic' procession included a tribe of Royal gypsies and two Zulus who appeared in the 'fantastic garb of their country'. Two bands provided music for dancing outside during the day and at night in the large ballrooms.

43　The Abbey Lakes hotel and grounds were the focus of much social life and the celebrations associated with royal events were usually located there. Queen Victoria's Golden Jubilee in 1887 saw Up Hollanders inclined towards 'a general disposition to go mad' and to indulge 'in every sort of innocent buffoonery'. The villagers enjoyed the attractions of Abbey Lakes, which included the grounds, well-kept gardens, boating, dancing, music and firework display. In a decorated marquee, capable of holding four hundred people, meals of beef, mutton, potatoes, peas, cabbage, plum pudding, beer and mineral waters were laid on. After dusk 'an immense multitude' congregated to appreciate the coloured lamps and candles, which illuminated the streets through which a torchlight procession paraded at 11 p.m.

44 In the early hours of 9 April 1912 disaster struck Abbey Lakes. A fire completely gutted the pavilion and caused considerable damage to the bar and tea rooms; one of the 450 people who had spent Easter Monday at Abbey Lakes had left a lighted cigarette on the pavilion floor and the flames were fanned by strong winds during the night. In 1925 the owner invested a considerable amount of money in restoring Abbey Lakes Hotel and Pleasure Gardens as a 'pleasure resort'. The project included emptying and cleaning the lake, which had become foul and a danger to health. The scheme received a big boost with the opening of the new Dance Hall with 4,000 square feet of maple floor and a full band in attendance. Later in the same year the first annual brass band contest was held in the grounds.

45 Trams from Wigan brought visitors to Abbey Lakes and provided services for local people. But the service was not always satisfactory. There was no shelter for passengers waiting for trams at Abbey Lakes and lighting was inadequate; it was claimed that two electric arc lights were needed to obviate the danger arising from the taking off of the trolley before the passengers alighted. Up Hollanders also complained about high fares and the unreliability of the service. In 1925 workmen who needed to be in Wigan for the 5.15 a.m. train could not rely on the 4.45 a.m. tram from Abbey Lakes and they were forced to walk two miles to Lamberhead Green to catch a more reliable car. In 1910 the driver and conductor of the tramway company were suspected of being implicated in street betting at the Abbey Lakes terminus, running bets for Up Holland men.

46   In 1933 Wigan and District Regional Town Planning Committee scheduled Dean Wood as an 'open space' but its natural attractions have been threatened. In June 1861 it was hit by a whirlwind that caused extensive damage. Large trees were torn up and others with firmer roots were snapped like reeds. The North Ashton Botanical Society visited Dean Wood to inspect the damage and to examine and collect some of the rare and beautiful specimens. In 1921 Kill Devil Bridge was in a dangerous condition and the wooden bridge replaced with a metal and concrete structure with a 30 feet span. In the following year a landslide in the vicinity of this bridge led the huge stones, which formed the footpath, to slip leaving a gaping chasm, which was potentially fatal to children and highly dangerous to adults.

47 The Ashurst Beacon was another Up Holland beauty spot. The original stone and wooden building was erected in 1701 to give early warning of possible enemy invasions; an alarm fire could be seen on a clear day by ships in the Irish Sea and by people as far away as Wales, Yorkshire and Cumberland. But the main role of Ashurst Beacon has always been for recreation. During the 1930s riders and the hounds of the Holcombe Hunt met at Ashurst Beacon. The celebrations of many royal events climaxed with the lighting of a bonfire on Ashurst Beacon; on the night of 21 June 1887 Ashurst Beacon was part of a chain of beacons illuminated in honour of Queen Victoria's Golden Jubilee. At Easter and Whit holidays all routes to the Beacon were crowded with pedestrians.

48   It was not always peaceful at Ashurst Beacon. In 1875, when the landlord of the Prince William Hotel threatened to eject two noisy coal miners, one of them kicked out with his iron-tipped pit clogs; the landlord subsequently died and the miner was charged with manslaughter. However, most visitors to the Beacon came to appreciate its beauty. In 1905 members of the Liverpool Geological Association spent a full day at the Beacon, which they found of 'great interest to the student of geology, and not without attraction to a lover of natural scenery'. During the 1920s the Prince William was the terminus for buses bringing visitors to enjoy the views from Ashurst Beacon. The route was via Hall Green and along Mill Lane with buses every 40 minutes, the last service leaving the Prince William Hotel terminus at 9.20 p.m.

49 Cricket was an integral part of the sporting and social scene in Up Holland. At a match in 1862 the ground 'presented a very animated appearance'. Several of the ladies of the village 'honoured the players with their presence'. The youngsters who crowded the adjoining land 'added very much to the merriment of the spectators by getting up races'. The game was followed by liquid refreshment at the White Lion. But it was not always such an idyllic scene. In 1884 there was controversy when Hindley All Saints defeated Up Holland. There were complaints about the 'disgusting utterance' of the Up Holland spectators. The Up Holland club denied any such discourtesy: 'It is no part of our need to publish the shortcomings or meanness of our opponents... by screening them we shall show the Hindley saints what Up Holland sinners can do.'

50 The Council congratulated Up Holland Athletic Football Club on the double success in the 1933 season, when finishing top of the Juvenile Organisation Committee Welfare League and winning the Broughton Cup. In the League they won 21 out of 28 games and lost only 3, going undefeated after Christmas. Their home matches on the sports field in Back School Lane were watched by large crowds and they played fast, open football, scoring 111 goals and conceding only 33. The Cup Final was played at Mount Zion Ground in Pemberton and after a hard fought game Up Holland won by two goals to one, St. Patrick's missing the chance to equalise with a penalty with just two minutes to play. After the match Alderman McCurdy presented the Broughton Cup and the Rushton Bowl (for the League Championship) to the Up Holland captain.

51 When the Council discussed the provision of children's playgrounds in the 1920s, it approached Squire Bankes, a major landowner in Up Holland. One field towards Tower Hill was considered to be neither very level nor very convenient for the main part of the village. Another piece of land near Brooklands House would have been nearer the heart of the village, where most children lived, but its undulating nature made it less than suitable as a playground. The search continued because playing fields were seen as a means of keeping younger children off the public streets and of providing exercise in the open air. Applications were made to the National Playing Fields Association and the Carnegie United Kingdom Trust for grants, but there was little progress because of the large expenditure involved.

WINSTANLEY HALL

52 The scattered nature of Up Holland made it difficult to make playfield provision in all areas, but Digmoor had a generous benefactor. William Mack had been Headmaster of Digmoor School from 1874 until his retirement in 1920. As a memorial to their father's work, his two sons purchased over 3 acres of land for a recreation ground. On 25 August 1937 the Mack Playing Field was officially handed over by the Mack family to Up Holland Urban District Council, which undertook to support and maintain the playground and to equip it with recreational appliances. Mr. J. Perry Jones, Secretary of the Lancashire Playing Fields Association, hoped that it would do much to improve the stamina of local children and that adolescents who laboured in the mills and workshops would have similar provision made for their recreation.

53   Important families in Up Holland frequently arranged events in support of worthy causes and these were major social occasions. In 1912 Councillor Wilcock and his family of Sea View House hosted a garden party in aid of funds for the enlargement and improvement of the church schools. Encouraged by delightful weather, large numbers of friends and relatives turned up to participate in the lawn tennis, bowls and competitions. The coach house was transformed into a concert room, which was twice crowded to enjoy the musical treat provided by the artistes. The lady palmist in her gypsy tent proved a great attraction with most of the guests, especially the gentlemen. Miss Wilcock produced a cookery book, containing over two hundred useful recipes. In the opinion of some, Up Holland had never had a more enjoyable social party.

Garden Party at Upholland.
In Aid of Church Schools' Enlargement Fund.

54 In 1865 the old Up Holland Grammar School hosted a meeting in support of a reading room and library for the diffusion of useful knowledge; it was felt that this would raise them 'in the scale of society'. They rented a building in School Lane, which was available every day of the week, except Sundays, when it was used as a chapel. The reading room was open from 10 a.m. to 10 p.m. and contained a collection of daily and weekly newspapers and magazines including The Times, The Telegraph, The Standard, Manchester Guardian, Liverpool Mercury, Wigan Observer, Wigan Examiner, Warrington Guardian, Illustrated London News and Punch. The library was open once or twice each week; for a small charge members could borrow from the two hundred books on show. A series of 'penny readings' proved very popular and attracted large attentive audiences.

55 This picture of John 'Dolly' Mills lighting lamps from his donkey-drawn cart was accepted and commended by Queen Alexandra. Years earlier, in 1863, the wedding of the then Princess Alexandra to the Prince of Wales, later King Edward VII, was celebrated with gusto in Up Holland. The Parish Church bells were rung and five large flags were hoisted on the tower. A brass band accompanied the children's procession through the village. In the evening a large coal bonfire, funded by public subscriptions, was ignited. To add to the illumination from the fire, almost every cottage window was lit up with candles. The coronation of King Edward VII and Queen Alexandra in 1902, scheduled for June, had to be postponed until August because of the King's illness and many events were 'shorn of their splendour and gaiety'.

56 For the coronation of King George V and Queen Mary in 1911 Up Holland glowed from end to end with colourful flags, streamers and decorated arches across the main streets. In the morning the ringers rang several peals of the church bells. Dignitaries in 'a carriage and pair' headed the official procession from Hall Green. Throughout the day the Do Da Band and the Pemberton Total Abstinence Band provided the entertainment. At night the charming decorations were illuminated by Chinese lanterns and Up Holland's biggest ever crowd assembled to witness the illuminations, the firework display near the old windmill and the torchlight parade through the village. Beautifully decorated wagons carried the children in their festival clothes, accompanied by a band in bright uniforms.

57   Up Holland streets were gaily decorated and large crowds gathered to celebrate the Silver Jubilee of King George V and Queen Mary in 1935. A large procession, which included nine hundred school children, assembled at Hall Green and proceeded along the main streets of the village, accompanied by the Wigan British Legion Band, the Pemberton Old Prize Band and the Up Holland British Legion Do Da Band. The main celebrations were held in the Abbey Lakes grounds and hall. In the after-noon the children competed in inter-school sports. After tea the Jolly Boys from Bolton gave a concert in the Dance Hall and Councillor Ernest Swift lit a huge bonfire. The evening reached its climax with the Jubilee dance.

58 The coronation of King George VI and Queen Elizabeth in 1937 provided another memorable day for the dignitaries and people of Up Holland. Having assembled at Hall Green the procession passed through the village en route for the Abbey Lakes Pleasure Gardens. Inter-schools sports occupied the afternoon before the children were entertained to tea in the large hall and a concert given by the Joy Boys. The Parr Public Brass Band, the Pemberton Old Prize Band and the village Do Da Jazz Band entertained throughout the day. The Coronation Ball was held in the Dance Pavilion with music provided by Doris Draper and her seven-piece dance orchestra. In preparation for the celebrations council workmen had collected timber from local works and from the demolished Legs of Man inn to create a huge bonfire, which was ignited by Councillor Swift.

THE UP HOLLAND
Programme of Festivities
ON THE OCCASION OF
THE CORONATION
OF
Their Majesties King George VI
and Queen Elizabeth.

Wednesday, May 12th, 1937,
TO BE HELD AT THE
Abbey Lakes Pleasure Grounds
School Lane :: Up Holland

Price 1d.

59   In August 1904 Up Holland became the centre of interest as large crowds were attracted to the village by the manifestations of the Church Street ghost. The Manchester Guardian correspondent wrote: 'Search England through and you could not find a more ideal spot to locate a haunted house than Up Holland. It is a place of ancient houses and irregular architecture, and its narrow, winding streets are almost too steep for traffic.' Up Holland became 'quite a Mecca for psychical investigators' including Mr. W. E. Garrett Fisher, who believed 'one of the most characteristic and interesting types of ghost has made its appearance in the village of Up Holland'. In an article in the Daily Mail he put forward three possible explanations of the phenomenon; a person playing a practical joke, a poltergeist or spirit and a 'still unknown source'.

60 The ghost house was 'a place of massive walls, with deep window seats and low ceilings, oak raftered, while the doors swing at uneven angles'. The actual room where most ghostly activity took place was about four yards square with massive white-washed beams and hard plaster, which Archie Hunt called 'stave and daub'. The ghost was active between 10.30 p.m. and midnight with knockings and rumblings, paper torn off the walls, patches of plaster scattered about the room and stones flung to the floor. A policeman admitted: 'It passes my understanding, and I'm astounded.' People were allowed to view the chamber; one visitor declared that the 'eerie spectacle and ghostly scene' was sufficient to 'freeze the laughter on their lips'. Eventually Mrs. Winstanley, the occupant, stopped the visits: 'Folk will think it's a money making concern.'

61 Lady de Holland was actually village character John Winstanley alias 'John Dolly', who specialised in female impersonations. He was a master of make up and disguise; his costumes included button up leg gaters, hats, stoles, shawls and voluminous knickers. Especially after a few drinks, he would stand on a stone 'pulpit' opposite the Old Dog inn, dressed as Mrs. Pankhurst, and poke fun at women in general and suffragettes in particular in speeches, which were a mix of politics, humour and bad language. He was also a member of the Do Da band, which attended most of the social functions in the village. John Dolly was also a great practical joker and he was suspected of having some involvement in the mysterious activities associated with the ghost house.

62   Up Holland's pubs were centres of social activity but they also had other functions. At the Old Dog inn an inquest was held in 1884 on a fatal accident at Crow Orchard Colliery, where a young miner was killed by a large stone that fell from the roof. In the same year the Old Dog was used for an inquiry into the death of an Irish farm labourer strangled at a lodging house on Alma Hill. In 1858 Jenkinson's field in Pimbo Lane was the scene of a bare knuckle fight that went on for more than an hour as the two men fought over about thirty rounds for a £5 bet made in the pub. About four hundred or five hundred spectators watched the fight and when local farmers and householders became alarmed by the mob the police were contacted; it took time to restore order and the crowd threatened to throw the policeman into a nearby pit!

63   Just prior to the Second World War, Dickinson's, a local building firm, submitted plans to Up Holland Urban District Council for a cinema in Grove Road. Planning permission was eventually granted, but with conditions: the builders were instructed to create a lay-by and a forecourt with two accesses to the lay-by. Work commenced on the cinema in February 1939, but on-site problems and disagreements over toilet provision delayed progress. Eventually a compromise was reached and the Lyric cinema was opened officially on 6 November 1939. Like many small cinemas, it closed in the 1950s when it became impossible to compete with television; it was purchased by Up Holland Church as a parish hall before eventually assuming an industrial function.

64 Up Holland Parish Church has had its ups and downs over the centuries. In 1834 it was described as 'a fine old building, having a solid tower, over which ivy creeps, and renders it a highly picturesque object'. However, by 1875 a visitor called Up Holland Church 'the most neglected, cold and cheerless place of worship' and alterations to the interior were nothing short of 'acts of vandalism'. Lack of money was a problem: 'We want a thousand pound left us, and then we could do something.' Fortunately there was 'a yearning desire for an altered state of things'; a new chancel was designed by Basil Champneys in the 1880s. Nevertheless, another visitor in 1926 was depressed by the 'somewhat ruinous state' of the old tower, which seemed 'destined to fall unless speedily repaired'.

65 From her house opposite, Miss Weeton enjoyed watching children in the churchyard 'diverting themselves in many a harmless frolic'. There are many interesting epitaphs on gravestones especially in the old section; the new graveyard was consecrated by the Bishop of Liverpool in 1905. One of the most intriguing said: 'Here underneath thou dost approach, the body of John Smith, the coachman.' Ellen Weeton prepared a long epitaph for her mother, but the actual inscription on Mrs. Weeton's gravestone simply stated: 'Mary Weeton, died 5th December, 1797, aged 51.' From the words on her gravestone it was clear that another woman, Alice Lea, who died in 1869 aged 84, was a loving and caring mother:

Grieve not for me, my days are past,
So long for you my love did last

Grieve not for me, but comfort take
And love each other for my sake!

66 Up Holland Parish Church is known for the 'curious and quaint relics of its interior'. Rev. John Braithwaite from The Priory transformed Up Holland Grammar School into The Academy, a successful seminary; when he died suddenly in 1812 the social atmosphere of The Priory suffered, but his work was commemorated by a memorial on the south wall of the church. Braithwaite's son in law, Rev. John Bird, later ran the school and was Curate for 11 years and Perpetual Curate for 22 years at Up Holland. His friends erected a tablet in recognition of his aim 'to promote the truest interests of rich and poor' and his 'earnest desire to reside among his people'. There are also monuments to the local doctors, teachers and gentry, including members of the Bankes family of Winstanley Hall and the Bispham family from Bispham Hall.

67   Rev. Frederick George Wills, Vicar of Up Holland from 1888 until 1927, was another remembered by a plaque on the wall of the parish church. In addition to his pastoral duties, Rev. Wills, as a member of Up Holland Urban District Council, was active on the secular scene. During the First World War he was Chairman of the Up Holland District Military Tribunal and worked hard to support the families of soldiers and sailors; he visited hospitals and camps all over the country. Much of the work was done on his motor cycle and the Council supported his application for an increased supply of petrol. When peace returned Rev. Wills played a prominent role in raising funds for the erection of the War Memorial; he died on Good Friday, just a week before he was scheduled to give the dedication at the unveiling ceremony.

REV. C.F. WILLS

68 John William Bamforth succeeded his father, William, as Headmaster of the village school in 1898 and held the position until his retirement from the teaching profession in 1925. He was a highly respected member of Up Holland Urban District Council and had been elected Chairman just before his death in May 1929. Amongst other duties he represented the Council on the United Charities of Up Holland. Mr. Bamforth was a prominent member of Up Holland Parish Church where he served as organist, choirmaster, vestry clerk and secretary to the Church Council. A large congregation attended his funeral and the procession, which included representatives of the police, the churches and the Council, was watched by large numbers of sympathetic villagers along the whole route to the Parish Church.

69 Great efforts were made on behalf of the church schools in Up Holland, but academic progress was retarded by a number of factors. Some parents neglected to send their children to school. Sickness and severe weather affected attendance and children often missed school at harvest, potato picking or blackberry seasons. Mondays were traditionally bad for attendance because 'many of the children go to Wigan'. However, the report by the Government Inspectors on the village schools in 1930 indicated that these difficulties were being overcome: 'Conveyance to a stranger of what has been learnt, ease and happiness in the exchange of ideas and ideals, these have been actually the main difficulty to be surmounted by children in country schools, and it is excellent that it is precisely in these aspects that a visitor notices happy progress.'

70   In 1907, Lancashire Education Committee felt that it was 'inadvisable' for the Up Holland Grammar School to continue to exist as a secondary school, but local inhabitants raised a petition stating that the school was 'very necessary' in the interests of those who desired secondary education in the neighbourhood. Since 1902 it had shared with other schools in Up Holland in providing technical instruction at evening classes in hygiene, ambulance, nursing, needlework, dressmaking, millinery, cookery, shorthand, English, mathematics, chemistry, mining, magnetism and electricity. But technical education was not cheap. In 1918 an evening typewriting class with 38 students had only one machine; the teacher was refused more typewriters because of the 'excessive costs' and was instructed to confine the class to shorthand.

71 During the First World War Saint Joseph's College was virtually at a standstill as many students joined the forces. With peace, College life returned to normal and there was an influx of both Senior and Junior students. To accommodate the increased numbers of students and to enable them to have complete uninterrupted training it was considered necessary to enlarge the College. The inspiration for the extension came from Archbishop Francis Keating. Between 1923 and 1930 there was almost continuous development and expansion of the College, including the North Wing, the new East Wing, the South Wing and the new Chapel, planned by Purcell. The extensions were built in red sandstone, brought in from Prescot, Rainhill and Woolton, which contrasts with the darker local stone of the original building.

72 The initial plan was to have one lake in the grounds of Saint Joseph's College, but when digging began in 1900 technical difficulties meant that water entering at the higher level simply ran out at the lower end because of the variations in the level of the land. Hence the decision was taken to make the original lake smaller and by building a dam to control the water, and thus to create a second lake at a lower level. Students at the College completed most of the physical labour; it was hard and demanding work, especially during spells of wet weather when the site became a sea of mud. The final stage involved 'puddling' clay on the bed of the lakes in order to prevent loss of water; both lakes were completed by 1907.

73   Saint Joseph's College was described in the College Magazine (1931) as 'the place with all the woods'. According to the writer: 'Almost every shade of green is there, from the pine trees lit with their flickering candles, toning slowly into a holly, softening into the green of a hawthorn, growing paler in a sycamore and chestnut, becoming translucently vivid in a beech, and then growing suddenly dark again in a kirtle of rhododendrons, caught up with blossoms, and extending right down to the water's edge.' Other highlights of the grounds included the disused quarry with 'gorse aflame' and the 'sea of bluebells' each May.

74 The foundation stone for the new Primitive Methodist Church at Roby Mill was laid in 1860 and replaced a building, which had been rented for services for 16 years but which had proved totally inadequate for the demand; a number of children had to be refused admission to the Sunday School because of lack of space. The new chapel, which was 36 feet long and 27 feet wide, could seat a congregation of 150. Church members who worked in the local quarries furnished and dressed the stone used in the building. The cost of the new chapel was £150 and this was met after a prolonged programme of fund raising activities. In 1929 an acre of land opposite the chapel was purchased and in 1937 a new Sunday School was erected on it; built of Ravenhead rustic brick at a cost of £1,300 it could accommodate a congregation of up to three hundred people.

75   Joseph Boyers lived for 72 years in Tontine, which he considered to be 'the nicest place on earth'. He began work in the coalmines when he was 10 years of age. In public life he was a respected member of Up Holland Urban District Council and of the Wigan Board of Guardians. But he was best remembered for his active association with the religious life of Tontine, where he had a major influence on the lives of hundreds of young people. For sixty years he was a leading member of the Tontine United Methodist Church as superintendent of the Sunday School, class leader, trustee, preacher and organist. He was also a devoted worker in the Christian Endeavour movement. The impressive turnout for his funeral at Tontine Methodist Chapel and at Up Holland Parish Church in August 1928 was an indication of the respect in which he was held.

76 The Abbey House, home of the Hunts for many years, was an important centre of social life and many events in aid of worthy causes were supported by the family. In August 1920 a gala in aid of Up Holland Parish Church funds was held on the cricket field; prizes were awarded to the best exhibitors in the show. In 1929 a garden fete was hosted in support of the Parish Church Lighting Fund; in addition to a whist drive and other games, the fortune telling provided 'ample amusement' whilst the Abbeyville Troupe 'entertained gaily'. By the end of the year Up Holland Parish Church was lighted with electricity for the first time. During the Second World War the villagers were invited to buy tea tickets to attend garden parties and bring and buy sales to boost the Up Holland Village Comforts Fund and the Methodist Church Comforts Fund.